# Shall we dance?

*Shall we*

EIGHT CLASSIC
BALLROOM DANCES
IN EIGHT
QUICK LESSONS

*dance?*

BY

MANINE ROSA GOLDEN

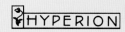

Copyright © 1997 by Marquand Books

Concept by Ed Marquand

Text by Manine Rosa Golden

Design by Brian Ellis Martin and Noreen Ryan

Dance Technique Consultant: Michael Wachel

Flip Book Dancers: Susan and Fred Telewski

Except those on the title page and page 1, all photos
courtesy of Photofest, New York, New York

Library of Congress Cataloging-in-Publication Data

Golden, Manine Rosa, 1969–

      Shall we dance? : eight classic ballroom dances in eight quick

  lessons / Manine Rosa Golden.

        p.    cm.

      ISBN 0-7868-8212-3

      1. Ballroom dancing—Study and teaching. I. Title.

  GV1753.5.G65  1997

  793.3'3—DC20                    96-20585

First edition

10 9 8 7 6 5 4 3 2 1

Printed in Hong Kong

# contents

# introduction

ANYONE CAN FAKE IT, BUT AREN'T YOU TIRED OF FUMBLING ACROSS THE DANCE FLOOR, STEPPING ON TOES IN FRONT OF YOUR FRIENDS AND FAMILY? FOR THOSE OF YOU WHO HAVE ALWAYS ADMIRED FINE DANCERS FROM AFAR BUT HAVE NEVER FOUND THE TIME TO PURSUE THE SKILL YOURSELVES, OR THOSE WHO JUST NEED A REFRESHER COURSE IN THE BASICS OF BALLROOM DANCING, NOW IS YOUR CHANCE! *SHALL WE DANCE?* WILL FAMILIARIZE YOU WITH THE BASIC STEPS OF THE EIGHT MOST POPULAR BALLROOM DANCES IN MINUTES. ONCE YOU'VE FOLLOWED THE INSTRUCTIONS IN THIS FUN AND EASY-TO-USE BOOK, YOU'LL QUICKLY DISCOVER THE SOCIAL, MENTAL, AND PHYSICAL BENEFITS OF BALLROOM DANCING. IT'S SO EASY TO LEARN, AND HARD TO FORGET.

YOU'LL BE GLIDING ACROSS THE FLOOR IN NO TIME. AND THE NEXT TIME YOU ARE AT A WEDDING, YOU CAN TURN TO YOUR PARTNER WITH CONFIDENCE AND ASK, "SHALL WE DANCE?"

# how to use this book

THIS BOOK IS DIVIDED INTO EIGHT SECTIONS, ONE FOR EACH DANCE. EACH SECTION BEGINS WITH A DESCRIPTION OF THE DANCE AND ITS ORIGINS, THEN PROVIDES AN EASY-TO-READ DIAGRAM OF THE DANCE, AND A CONCISE EXPLANATION OF EACH STEP INVOLVED. TOGETHER, THESE STEPS FORM THE BASIC *FIGURE* OF THE DANCE. AFTER THE BASIC FIGURE INSTRUCTION IS A SECTION THAT EXPLAINS HOW TO REPEAT THE FIGURE FLUIDLY. THE REPETITION OF THE FIGURES IS CALLED AN *AMALGAMATION*.

BEFORE YOU START TO LEARN THE DANCE STEPS IN THIS BOOK, IT IS A GOOD IDEA TO STUDY THE DIAGRAM FIRST, THEN READ THE INSTRUCTIONS. USE YOUR FINGERS ON THE FOOTPRINT DIAGRAMS, PRETENDING THAT YOUR INDEX AND MIDDLE FINGERS ARE YOUR LEFT AND RIGHT FEET. THIS WILL HELP YOU TO VISUALIZE AND MEMORIZE THE STEPS IN THE FIGURE. ONCE YOU'RE COMFORTABLE DANCING YOUR STEPS ALONE, DANCE WITH A PARTNER. BOTH PARTNERS'

STEPS ARE REPRODUCED ON THE SAME PAGE SO THAT YOU CAN FOLLOW IN-STRUCTIONS AND LEARN TOGETHER.

WHEN YOU GO DANCING IN PUBLIC, YOU MAY NOTICE THAT OTHER COUPLES DANCE THE SAME DANCE DIFFERENTLY. THERE ARE MANY SCHOOLS OF DANCE, AND EACH HAS A UNIQUE APPROACH TO THE INDIVIDUAL DANCES. THAT IS THE WONDER OF BALLROOM DANCE! ENJOY IT. IF YOU SEE A COUPLE DANCING THE FOXTROT DIFFERENTLY THAN YOU, AND IF YOU LIKE THEIR APPROACH BETTER, ASK THEM ABOUT IT.

# before you begin

EACH COUPLE IS MADE UP OF A *LEADER* AND A *FOLLOWER*. THE LEADER DECIDES THE FIGURES TO DANCE AND THEIR ORDER. THE FOLLOWER, NORMALLY UNAWARE OF WHICH FIGURE THE LEADER WILL CHOOSE, MUST BE ABLE TO FOLLOW BASED ON THE LEADER'S SUGGESTIONS. THE LEADER LEADS THROUGH THE DISTRIBUTION OF WEIGHT. FOR EXAMPLE, IN ORDER TO STEP FORWARD WITH THE RIGHT FOOT, WEIGHT MUST FIRST BE SETTLED ON THE LEFT FOOT. THE FOLLOWER MUST RESPOND TO THIS DISTRIBUTION OF WEIGHT, INFERRING WHAT THE NEXT STEP WILL BE. AS A LEADER, IT IS IMPORTANT TO COMMUNICATE THE DANCE PLAN CLEARLY AND CONFIDENTLY. AS A FOLLOWER, IT IS IMPORTANT NOT TO RESIST.

BASIC BALLROOM DANCE STEPS CAN BE BROKEN DOWN INTO EITHER *WALKING* STEPS OR *SIDE* STEPS. ALL OF THE DANCES IN THIS BOOK ARE COMPOSED OF THESE STEPS OR A VARIATION OF THEM. WALKING STEPS ARE TAKEN EITHER FORWARD OR BACKWARD. WHEN WALKING FORWARD, THE HEEL HITS THE FLOOR

FIRST, FOLLOWED BY THE BALL OF THE FOOT. WHEN WALKING BACKWARD, THE TOE HITS THE FLOOR FIRST, THEN ROLLS TO THE BALL AND HEEL OF THE FOOT. SIDE STEPS ARE TAKEN ON THE BALLS OF THE FEET, THEN LOWERED TO THE HEELS AS THE FEET COME TOGETHER.

THERE ARE TWO STYLES OF DANCE INCLUDED IN THIS BOOK: *SMOOTH* AND *RHYTHM*. A SMOOTH DANCE IS ANY DANCE THAT PROGRESSES AROUND THE DANCE FLOOR, INCLUDING THE FOXTROT, WALTZ, AND TANGO. RHYTHM DANCES ARE THOSE THAT ARE DANCED IN PLACE, LIKE THE CHA-CHA, SAMBA, SWING, RUMBA, AND MAMBO.

FOR SIMPLICITY'S SAKE, WE USE ONE STANCE, OR *HOLD*, IN THIS BOOK TO DESCRIBE THE POSTURE AND POSITION PARTNERS SHOULD BE IN WHILE DANCING. THIS IS THE *CLOSED HOLD*. IN THE CLOSED HOLD, FACING ONE ANOTHER, THE LEADER'S RIGHT HAND RESTS ON THE FOLLOWER'S BACK, BELOW THE LEFT SHOULDER BLADE. THE LEADER HOLDS THE FOLLOWER'S RIGHT HAND IN HIS

LEFT, AT CHIN LEVEL, BOTH ELBOWS BENT AND HELD SLIGHTLY AWAY FROM THE BODY. THE FOLLOWER'S RIGHT HIP SHOULD BE SLIGHTLY TO HER LEFT OF THE LEADER'S LEFT HIP. IN THE SMOOTH DANCES, PARTNERS SHOULD STAND A FEW INCHES APART. IN THE RHYTHM DANCES, THEY SHOULD STAND ONE TO TWO FEET APART IN THE SAME HOLD. BOTH PARTNERS SHOULD ALWAYS STAND STRAIGHT. THE STARTING POSITION FOR EACH STEP IN THIS BOOK IS WITH BOTH FEET TOGETHER.

ON THE DANCE FLOOR, YOUR CHOICE OF DANCE WILL BE DICTATED BY THE RHYTHM AND TEMPO (OR SPEED) OF THE MUSIC. MOST DANCE MUSIC IS WRITTEN IN 4/4, OR COMMON, TIME. THIS MEANS THAT THERE ARE FOUR BEATS PER MEASURE OF MUSIC. IN THE FOXTROT OR SWING, THE EMPHASIZED BEATS IN A FOUR-BEAT MEASURE ARE THE FIRST AND THIRD BEATS. IN LATIN AMERICAN DANCES, LIKE THE MAMBO, THE EMPHASIZED BEATS IN A FOUR-BEAT MEASURE ARE USUALLY THE SECOND AND FOURTH BEATS, AND THE FIRST BEAT IS OFTEN

A PAUSE. SOME MUSIC IS WRITTEN IN 3/4 TIME, MEANING THERE ARE THREE BEATS PER MEASURE. THIS IS MUSIC TO WHICH ONE CAN WALTZ.

IN SMOOTH DANCES, *QUICK* AND *SLOW* STEPS MAKE UP THE DANCE SEQUENCE. QUICK STEPS TAKE ONE BEAT AND SLOW STEPS TAKE TWO BEATS. THE STEPS ARE INTERSPERSED THROUGHOUT A DANCE, SO IN A FOUR-BEAT MEASURE OF MUSIC, THE STEPS MIGHT READ "QUICK, QUICK, SLOW" OR "SLOW, SLOW." THE TIMING OF RHYTHM DANCE STEPS IS DIFFERENT. TO MAKE THE RHYTHM STEPS EASIER TO UNDERSTAND, WE HAVE GIVEN THE STEPS AND BEATS NUMBERS INSTEAD OF USING THE TERMS *QUICK* AND *SLOW*.

WHEN DANCING IN PUBLIC WITH OTHER COUPLES, PARTNERS SHOULD DANCE ALONG THE *LINE OF DANCE*. THE LINE OF DANCE IS AN INVISIBLE COUNTERCLOCKWISE PATH AROUND THE DANCE FLOOR. COUPLES SHOULD ALWAYS TRAVEL IN THIS DIRECTION IN ORDER TO MAINTAIN A CONTINUOUS FLOW OF DANCE AND PREVENT COLLISIONS.

WHAT SHOULD YOU WEAR WHEN YOU GO DANCING? PROFESSIONAL BALLROOM DANCERS ARE FAMOUS FOR THEIR EXTENSIVE AND ELABORATE WARDROBES. WHILE WE ENCOURAGE YOU TO DRESS UP AND HAVE FUN, MAKE SURE THAT YOU ARE COMFORTABLE AND UNENCUMBERED. WEAR CLOTHES THAT PERMIT FREEDOM OF MOVEMENT. WOMEN MAY PREFER TO WEAR HEELS WHEN DANCING, TO HELP KEEP THE WEIGHT OF THE BODY FORWARD, ON THE BALLS OF THE FEET, WHERE MOST OF THE DANCE STEPS TAKE PLACE. MEN SHOULD WEAR FLEXIBLE, THIN-SOLED SHOES WITH A SLIGHT HEEL. AGAIN, THE HEEL HELPS TO KEEP BODY WEIGHT FORWARD. NO MATTER WHAT SHOES YOU DECIDE TO WEAR, THEY SHOULD BE COMFORTABLE AND FLEXIBLE.

*"Shall we*

*dance?"*

# foxtrot

THE FOXTROT IS THE WORLD'S MOST COMMONLY PERFORMED DANCE, SO IT'S A GOOD ONE TO KNOW. IT'S ALSO EASY TO LEARN. THE FOXTROT CAN BE DANCED TO MANY TYPES OF MUSIC IN 4/4 TIME. PARTNERS SHOULD BE IN THE CLOSED HOLD POSITION.

BEGIN THE FOXTROT WITH THE LEADER FACING DOWN THE LINE OF DANCE ANGLED AT ABOUT 45 DEGREES INTO THE WALL ON THE LEADER'S RIGHT SIDE. ONCE YOU MASTER THE FOXTROT, THE WALTZ, SWING, AND MANY LATIN DANCES WILL COME TO YOU MORE EASILY.

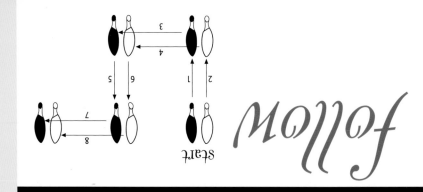

follow

start

lead

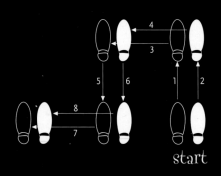

start

1. RIGHT FOOT BACK — Slow
2. LEFT FOOT BACK — Slow
3. RIGHT FOOT TO SIDE — Quick
4. LEFT FOOT CLOSES TO RIGHT FOOT — Quick
5. RIGHT FOOT FORWARD — Slow
6. LEFT FOOT FORWARD — Slow
7. RIGHT FOOT TO SIDE — Quick
8. LEFT FOOT CLOSES TO RIGHT FOOT — Quick

1. LEFT FOOT FORWARD — SLOW
2. RIGHT FOOT FORWARD — SLOW
3. LEFT FOOT TO SIDE — QUICK
4. RIGHT FOOT CLOSES TO LEFT FOOT — QUICK
5. LEFT FOOT BACK — SLOW
6. RIGHT FOOT BACK — SLOW
7. LEFT FOOT TO SIDE — QUICK
8. RIGHT FOOT CLOSES TO LEFT FOOT — QUICK

foxtrot

fox

# trot

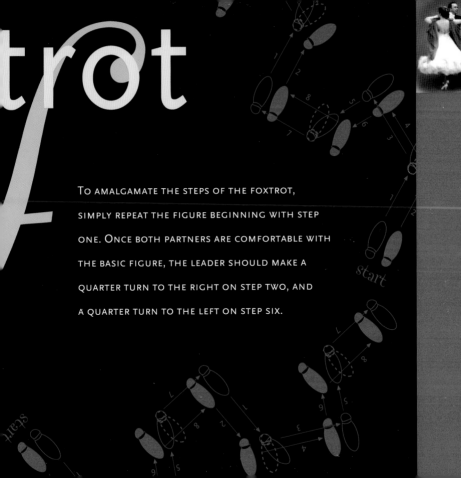

TO AMALGAMATE THE STEPS OF THE FOXTROT,
SIMPLY REPEAT THE FIGURE BEGINNING WITH STEP
ONE. ONCE BOTH PARTNERS ARE COMFORTABLE WITH
THE BASIC FIGURE, THE LEADER SHOULD MAKE A
QUARTER TURN TO THE RIGHT ON STEP TWO, AND
A QUARTER TURN TO THE LEFT ON STEP SIX.

start

$i$N ONE FORM OR ANOTHER, THE WALTZ HAS BEEN PERFORMED LONGER THAN ANY OTHER SOCIAL DANCE. AS WITH THE FOXTROT, UNDERSTANDING THE WALTZ WILL MAKE OTHER DANCES EASIER TO LEARN. WALTZ MUSIC IS IN 3/4 TIME,

MEANING THERE ARE THREE BEATS PER MEASURE OF MUSIC. EACH BEAT OF WALTZ MUSIC RECEIVES ONE DANCE STEP. THE FIRST BEAT OF THE WALTZ CARRIES THE EMPHASIS AND CORRESPONDS TO A FORWARD OR BACKWARD WALKING STEP IN THE BASIC SEQUENCE. THE CLEAR, SIMPLE STEPS OF THE WALTZ PRODUCE A SMOOTH PATTERN THAT WILL ALLOW YOU TO GLIDE GENTLY AROUND THE DANCE FLOOR IN NO TIME.

BE AWARE OF THE RISE-AND-FALL MOTIONS OF THE WALTZ STEPS. IN THE SIDE STEPS OF THE WALTZ, DANCERS SHOULD RAISE THEIR BODIES SLIGHTLY USING THE ANKLES AND ARCHES OF THE FEET. WALKING STEPS SHOULD BE TAKEN FIRMLY ON THE HEELS AND BALLS OF THE FEET. THE LEADER SHOULD FACE DOWN THE LINE OF DANCE ANGLED SLIGHTLY TOWARD THE WALL ON THE LEADER'S RIGHT SIDE. THE WALTZ SHOULD BE DANCED IN A CLOSED HOLD.

waltz

follow

start

lead

1. Left foot forward — Quick
2. Right foot to side — Quick
3. Left foot closes to right foot — Quick
4. Right foot forward — Quick
5. Left foot to side — Quick
6. Right foot closes to left foot — Quick

Waltz

1. Right foot back — Quick
2. Left foot to side — Quick
3. Right foot closes to left foot — Quick
4. Left foot back — Quick
5. Right foot to side — Quick
6. Left foot closes to right foot — Quick

wa

start

1

2

3

5

4

6

5

7

2

3

4

6

7

2

3

4

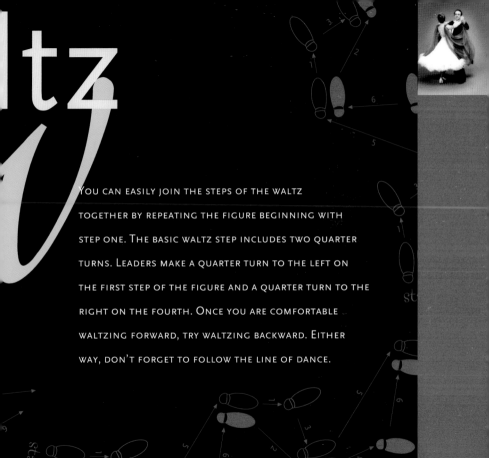

You can easily join the steps of the waltz together by repeating the figure beginning with step one. The basic waltz step includes two quarter turns. Leaders make a quarter turn to the left on the first step of the figure and a quarter turn to the right on the fourth. Once you are comfortable waltzing forward, try waltzing backward. Either way, don't forget to follow the line of dance.

# tango

The tango reflects the passionate, exciting music to which it is danced. While there are many dazzling sequences that can be added to this dance, the basic steps are easy to learn. The drama of the dance lies in the smooth, florid execution of the steps and the slow, tense rhythms of the music. The five steps of the basic tango take place in eight beats of tango music, two measures of music in 4/4 time. Be conservative while learning this dance; do not exaggerate your movements. The tango—known as the dance of love—should be danced in a closed hold.

follow

start

1
2
3
4
5

lead

start

1
2
3
4
5

5. Right toe closes to left foot (no weight) — Slow
4. Left foot to side — Quick
3. Right foot back — Quick
2. Left foot back — Slow
1. Right foot back — Slow

1. Left foot forward — Slow
2. Right foot forward — Slow
3. Left foot forward — Quick
4. Right foot to side — Quick
5. Left toe closes to right foot (no weight) — Slow

tango

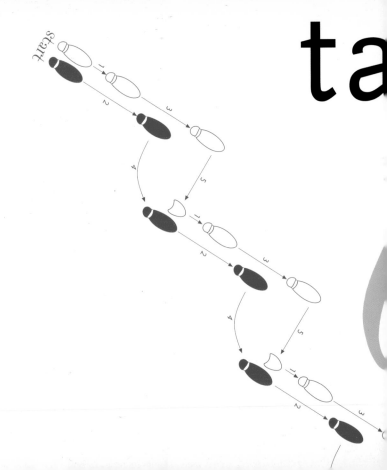

ta

# ngo

On the fifth step, when each partner closes to the standing foot, there is no weight shift when the feet come together. Each partner should rest the loose foot lightly on the ball only, ready to lift it again to repeat the sequence from step one.

*start*

*t*HE CHA-CHA, A DANCE DERIVED FROM THE CUBAN MAMBO, DEMANDS DELI-
CATE FOOTWORK AND FINESSE. WHILE THE CHA-CHA STEPS WILL BE EASIER BE-
CAUSE YOU NOW KNOW THE FOXTROT AND WALTZ, ITS RHYTHM IS SLIGHTLY

DIFFERENT. LIKE FOXTROT MUSIC, CHA-CHA MUSIC IS IN 4/4 TIME. BUT UNLIKE THE DANCES YOU'VE JUST LEARNED, THE COUNT OF THE CHA-CHA BEAT IS "TWO, THREE, FOUR AND, ONE," WITH "FOUR AND" FITTING INTO THE USUAL COUNT OF "FOUR" ALONE. THIS IS CALLED *TRIPLE TIME,* MEANING THAT THREE STEPS ARE TAKEN IN TWO BEATS, DESCRIBED AS "FOUR AND, ONE."

PARTNERS USE THE CLOSED HOLD IN THIS DANCE BUT, SINCE THE CHA-CHA IS A RHYTHM DANCE, THEY SHOULD STAND APPROXIMATELY ONE FOOT APART. CHA-CHA MUSIC IS CLEAN AND THE RHYTHMS ARE CLEAR. THE MOVEMENTS OF THE DANCE SHOULD BE SUBTLE BUT DELIBERATE, AND STEPS SHOULD BE SMALL AND PRECISE. WHILE THERE IS A CERTAIN AMOUNT OF WEIGHT SHIFTING IN THE CHA-CHA, DO NOT EXAGGERATE THE MOVEMENT OF THE HIPS. THE DANCE SHOULD BE ELEGANT, NOT AGGRESSIVE. THE CHA-CHA IS DANCED IN A SQUARE SPACE AND DOES NOT PROGRESS ALONG THE LINE OF DANCE.

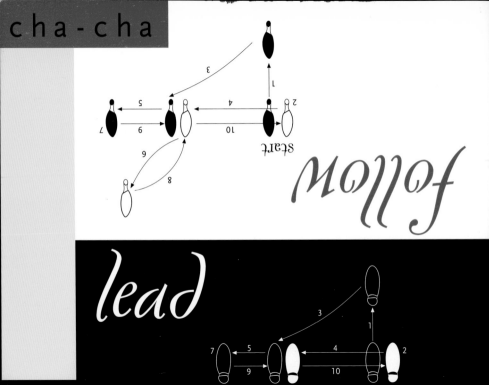

| | |
|---|---|
| 1. Right foot back | Two |
| 2. Left foot in place; weight shifts to it | Three |
| 3. Right foot to side | Four |
| 4. Left foot closes to right foot | And |
| 5. Right foot small step to side | One |
| 6. Left foot forward | Two |
| 7. Right foot in place; weight shifts to it | Three |
| 8. Left foot to side | Four |
| 9. Right foot closes to left foot | And |
| 10. Left foot small step to side | One |

| | |
|---|---|
| 1. Left foot forward | Two |
| 2. Right foot in place; weight shifts to it | Three |
| 3. Left foot to side | Four |
| 4. Right foot closes to left foot | And |
| 5. Left foot small step to side | One |
| 6. Right foot back | Two |
| 7. Left foot in place; weight shifts to it | Three |
| 8. Right foot to side | Four |
| 9. Left foot closes to right foot | And |
| 10. Right foot small step to side | One |

cha-cha

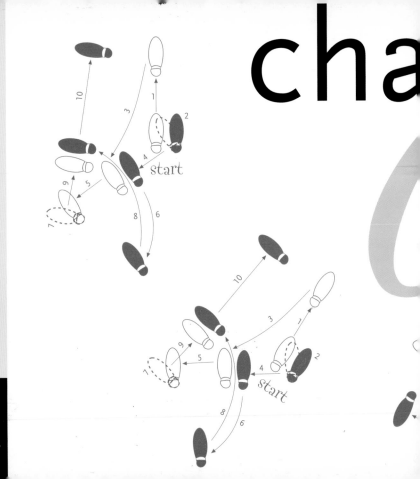

Amalgamate the figure by returning to step one from step ten. The leader can make a one-eighth turn to the left on steps two and seven for a simple variation.

Samba music, originally from Brazil, goes back hundreds of years and has a rich history. While there are many versions of the samba, most samba steps are done in *triple time*, meaning three steps are taken in two beats, described as "one and, two." This is similar to the cha-cha rhythm you just learned. Samba music is in 2/4 time, meaning there are only two beats per measure.

# samba

Samba steps are short, quick, and energetic, since the music is faster than the music for other dances we've described. The distinctive hip movement of the samba is created by stepping onto a straight, but not rigid, leg on the count of "one" (don't lock your knees!). The weight change on "and" is only partial, and is done on the toe of the closing foot with your knee bent. Finally, weight is shifted fully back to a straight, but not rigid, leg for the count of "two." There is very little bounce in the samba. The straight legs and partial weight change will help you achieve the hip movements that are an integral part of samba. Be careful not to exaggerate your movements, but let the hips move naturally as a result of the leg- and footwork. The samba should be danced in the closed hold with one to two feet of space between partners.

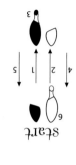

follow

lead

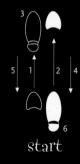

6. LEFT FOOT STAYS IN PLACE; WEIGHT SHIFTS TO IT — TWO
5. RIGHT TOE CLOSES TO LEFT FOOT — AND
4. LEFT FOOT FORWARD — ONE
3. RIGHT FOOT STAYS IN PLACE; WEIGHT SHIFTS TO IT — TWO
2. LEFT TOE CLOSES TO RIGHT FOOT — AND
1. RIGHT FOOT BACK — ONE

1. LEFT FOOT FORWARD — ONE
2. RIGHT TOE CLOSES TO LEFT FOOT — AND
3. LEFT FOOT STAYS IN PLACE; WEIGHT SHIFTS TO IT — TWO
4. RIGHT FOOT BACK — ONE
5. LEFT TOE CLOSES TO RIGHT FOOT — AND
6. RIGHT FOOT STAYS IN PLACE; WEIGHT SHIFTS TO IT — TWO

samba

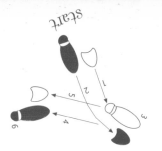

start

# sa

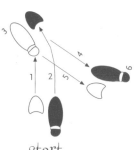

start

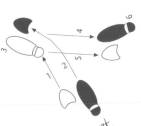

start

# mba

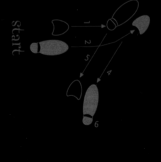

THE SAMBA FIGURE CAN BE REPEATED BY
RETURNING TO STEP ONE WHEN THE FIGURE
IS COMPLETE. THE LEADER CAN ADD A
SLIGHT TURN TO THE LEFT ON
STEPS ONE AND FOUR.

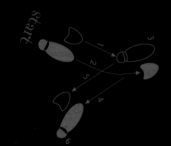

SWING IS A MODIFIED, MORE SOPHISTICATED VERSION OF THE JITTERBUG.
SWING RHYTHM FITS EIGHT STEPS INTO SIX BEATS OF MUSIC IN 4/4 TIME. THE
"ONE AND" AND THE "THREE AND" BEATS FIT INTO THE COUNTS OF "ONE" AND
"THREE," RESPECTIVELY. THE SIDE STEPS SHOULD BE TAKEN WITH BENT KNEES
AND A BOUNCE. WHEN STEPPING BACKWARD ON THE SEVENTH COUNT, BE CARE-
FUL NOT TO PULL TOO FAR AWAY FROM YOUR PARTNER. REMEMBER TO USE THE
BALL OF YOUR FOOT TO STEP BACKWARD INSTEAD OF YOUR HEEL. THE LEADER'S
LEFT HAND AND FOLLOWER'S RIGHT HAND DROP TO WAIST LEVEL FOR THIS
DANCE, AND PARTNERS SHOULD STAND ONE-HALF FOOT TO ONE FOOT APART
IN THE CLOSED HOLD.

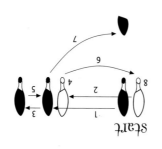

_follow_

start

_lead_

start

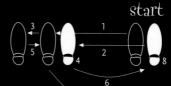

1. Right foot to side — One
2. Left foot closes to right foot — And
3. Right foot to side — Two
4. Left foot steps in place — Three
5. Right foot closes to left foot — And
6. Left foot to side — Four
7. Right foot back — Five
8. Left foot in place — Six

1. Left foot to side — One
2. Right foot closes to left foot — And
3. Left foot to side — Two
4. Right foot steps in place — Three
5. Left foot closes to right foot — And
6. Right foot to side — Four
7. Left foot back — Five
8. Right foot in place — Six

swing

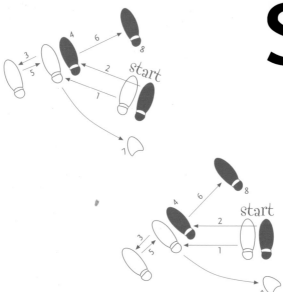

start

start

# SW

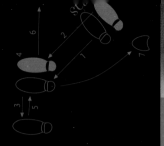

Repeat the swing figure by returning to step one from step eight. You can turn to the right or left on steps one through six, but no turn should be made on steps seven and eight.

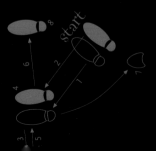

THE RUMBA ORIGINATED IN CUBA. ITS MOVES ARE REFINED, NOT OSTENTATIOUS, CONSISTING OF SUBTLE WEIGHT SHIFTS FOLLOWING EACH STEP. THE STEPS ARE SIMILAR TO THE "SLOW, QUICK, QUICK" STEPS OF THE SMOOTH DANCES, BUT ARE SHORT AND PRECISE LIKE THOSE OF THE CHA-CHA AND SAMBA. THE MUSIC IS IN 4/4 TIME. MAKE SURE THAT THE FIRST STEPS DANCED TO EACH MEASURE OF MUSIC ARE TAKEN ON THE FIRST BEAT. TAKE A MINUTE TO LISTEN TO RUMBA MUSIC AND PRACTICE PICKING UP THE BEATS BEFORE YOU BEGIN DANCING. THE STEP COMBINATIONS ARE CONFINED TO THE SQUARE AREA OF THE BASIC RUMBA BOX STEP AND DO NOT FOLLOW THE LINE OF DANCE. PARTNERS SHOULD STAND ABOUT ONE FOOT APART IN THE CLOSED HOLD.

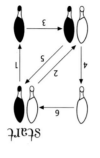

*follow*

start

*lead*

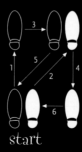

start

1. LEFT FOOT FORWARD — ONE, TWO
2. RIGHT FOOT TO SIDE — THREE
3. LEFT FOOT CLOSES TO RIGHT FOOT — FOUR
4. RIGHT FOOT BACK — ONE, TWO
5. LEFT FOOT TO SIDE — THREE
6. RIGHT FOOT CLOSES TO LEFT FOOT — FOUR

rumba

1. RIGHT FOOT BACK — ONE, TWO
2. LEFT FOOT TO SIDE — THREE
3. RIGHT FOOT CLOSES TO LEFT FOOT — FOUR
4. LEFT FOOT FORWARD — ONE, TWO
5. RIGHT FOOT TO SIDE — THREE
6. LEFT FOOT CLOSES TO RIGHT FOOT — FOUR

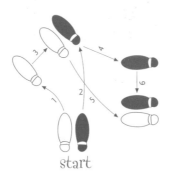

start

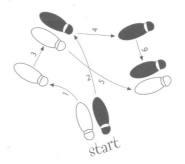

start

# ru

# mba

THE RUMBA BOX STEP CAN BE REPEATED FROM THE BEGINNING OF THE FIGURE, STARTING WITH STEP ONE. THE LEADER CAN ADD A ONE-EIGHTH TURN TO THE LEFT ON STEP ONE AND ANOTHER ONE-EIGHTH TURN TO THE LEFT ON STEP FOUR. AFTER FOUR QUARTER TURNS (OR EIGHT ONE-EIGHTH TURNS), YOU SHOULD END UP IN THE SAME PLACE YOU BEGAN.

Start

# mambo

THE MAMBO, A DANCE OF CUBA, SHOULD BE DANCED TO FAST MUSIC WITH A HEAVY BEAT. THE HIP MOVEMENT, WHETHER SIMPLE OR ELABORATE, IS ALWAYS PRONOUNCED, BUT THE STEPS ARE BASIC. THE 4/4 TIME OF THE MUSIC EMPHASIZES THE SECOND AND FOURTH BEATS, AND THERE IS A PAUSE ON THE FIRST BEAT. THE BEATS ARE "TWO, THREE, FOUR, ONE," AND THE STEPS ARE "QUICK, QUICK, SLOW" OR "STEP, STEP, STEP, PAUSE." TAKE A MINUTE TO LISTEN TO MAMBO MUSIC AND PRACTICE PICKING UP THE BEATS BEFORE YOU BEGIN DANCING. THE MAMBO IS DANCED IN A CLOSED POSITION. PARTNERS' CLASPED HANDS CAN BE HELD UP, HALF-WAY UP, OR DOWN, BUT ARMS AND HANDS SHOULD BE KEPT CLOSE TO THE BODY.

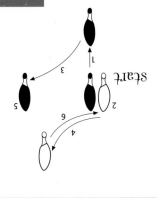

follow

start

3

1

2

6

4

5

lead

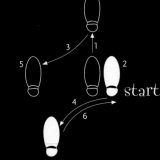

3

1

5

2

start

4

6

1. RIGHT FOOT BACK — TWO
2. LEFT FOOT STEPS IN PLACE — THREE
3. RIGHT FOOT SMALL STEP TO SIDE — FOUR, ONE
4. LEFT FOOT FORWARD — TWO
5. RIGHT FOOT STEPS IN PLACE — THREE
6. LEFT FOOT SMALL STEP TO SIDE — FOUR, ONE

1. LEFT FOOT FORWARD — TWO
2. RIGHT FOOT STEPS IN PLACE — THREE
3. LEFT FOOT SMALL STEP TO SIDE — FOUR, ONE
4. RIGHT FOOT BACK — TWO
5. LEFT FOOT STEPS IN PLACE — THREE
6. RIGHT FOOT SMALL STEP TO SIDE — FOUR, ONE

mambo

ma

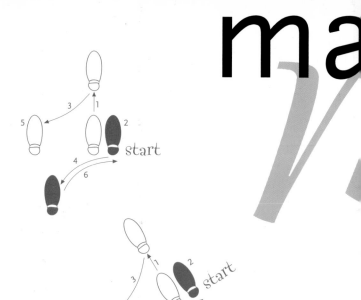

start

start

# mbo

To repeat the basic mambo step, simply
proceed directly from step six to step one
(without returning to the starting position, in which both feet are together).

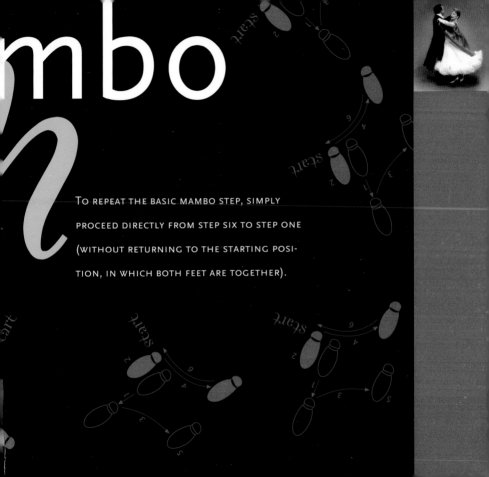

# a final word

Keep in mind that there are no "official" versions of each of the basic ballroom dances. Every teacher, every dance studio, has a different way of teaching. We have consulted a number of professional dance instructors and numerous books from a range of eras in order to provide you with steps that are easy to learn and maintain the character of each dance.

Once you have been through this book and realize how fun and easy ballroom dancing can be, we encourage you to take lessons and go out dancing with other couples. Watching others and learning from them will diversify your repertoire and increase your confidence. For information on where to find ballroom dance activities and instructors, contact the United States Amateur Ballroom Dancers Association at (800) 447-9047, or look in your local newspaper.